Daily Dexter-Flexers

technique builders for beginning keyboard students

Illustrations by Don Ezard

Exclusive distributors for Australia and New Zealand
Encore Music Distributors
227 Napier St, Fitzroy VIC 3065 Australia
Phone +61 3 9415 6677
Facsimile +61 3 9415 6655
Email sales@encoremusic.com.au

This book © Copyright 2014 by Margaret Brandman trading as Jazzem Music
46 Gerrale St, Cronulla NSW 2230 Australia
ISBN 978-0-949683-51-9
ISMN 979-0-720010-03-8
ORDER NUMBER MMP 8058
International copyright secured (APRA/AMCOS). All rights reserved.

Unauthorised reproduction of any part of this publication by any means,
including photocopying, is an infringement of copyright.

INTRODUCTION

The *Contemporary Piano Method* (CPM) is designed to equip the student with the necessary skills to play classical, contemporary popular, jazz and contemporary classical musical styles, with ease and understanding while giving experience in skills required for both classical and contemporary examination syllabi. The piano method is the central core of an integrated course which provides materials for ear-training (audio and workbooks), theory, improvisation, technique and repertoire.

Daily Dexter Flexers follows the *Junior Primer*, providing additional technique and reading practice to support books 1A and 1B of the Contemporary Piano Method. However the book can be used by both beginner level students (Level One) and those who have been playing for some time (Level Two).

By using the *Playing Made Easy* interval reading system, as shown in the method books, the exercises can be played in both written form by the beginner, or transposed into various keys by superimposing the interval patterns onto the keyboard pathways, by the advancing student. Dexter the koala (the CPM's symbol for dexterity) appears throughout the book to impart a more concrete meaning to the interval distances and direction concepts introduced in this book.

In order to transpose, the student merely needs to consider which end of the scale pattern is being used: lower or upper, adjust their fingers accordingly onto the correct black and white keys and continue reading by intervals. (Refer to *Pictorial Patterns for Keyboard Scales and Chords* or *CPM Book 1A* for the scale patterns.)

Direction Concepts
Using the gestalt (whole) view of interval movements and patterns, students are equipped to see a larger section of music in one glance, so that the combined direction of the notes for both hands becomes more obvious. Therefore many **similar** and **contrary** and **oblique** motions have been featured in the exercises, an area often neglected in traditional technique books.

Understanding the movements facilitates:
- the reading of two staves at once (the Grand Staff)
- the development of the pianist's ability to comprehend music for both hands in one thought
- awareness of musical shapes and patterns

The reading and learning process is simplified, enabling the student to become a music speed reader while at the same time developing facility.

Other features of this book are the drilling of the location of the five Cs as **signpost notes**, so that the starting notes for each of the exercises can be easily found and the use of timing diagrams to be coloured in and clapped. These help the student to quickly associate a concrete meaning to the language of music rhythm notation and establish a body feel for timing. The use of colour, spatial concepts and the tactile information transferred by the act of colouring brings into play many accelerated learning concepts.

Information on the interval and scale pattern approach can be found in the following integrated publications:

1. *Contemporary Piano Method – Junior Primer (JP) and Books 1A and 1B (CPM – 1A, CPM – 1B)*
2. *Contemporary Theory Primer (CTP)*
3. *Contemporary Theory Workbook – Book 1 (CTW – Book 1)*
4. *Contemporary Aural Course (audio and workbook series) – Preparatory Set, Set One and Set Two.* (CAC – Prep, CAC – 1 and CAC – 2)
5. *Pictorial Patterns for Keyboard Scales and Chords*

Look for the page references listed in *this* book.
Refer to the related books and audio each time a new interval is introduced so that the student has a thorough grasp of each concept.

For more detailed information on each of the materials refer to the website:
www.margaretbrandman.com

Margaret Brandman
Ph.D. (Mus/Arts) B.Mus., T.Mus.A., Hon.FNMSM.,
F.Mus.Ed.ASMC., F.Comp.ASMC.,
L.Perf.ASMC., A.Mus.A., ASA. T.Dip

International Woman of the Year for services to music 2003

CONTENTS

	TOPIC	PAGE
	General technique tips	4
	Counting, colouring, clapping	5
Group One	Steps (seconds)	6
	Whole, half and quarter notes	
	Similar and contrary motion	
Group Two	Skips (thirds) melodic and harmonic	11
	Sames (primes)	
	Eighth notes introduced	
	Legato vs staccato touch for steps together with repeated notes	
Group Three	Skip-plus-ones (fourths)	16
	Jumps (fifths)	
	Block & broken chord study	
Group Four	Sixths	19
	Scales – C and G majors	
	Thumb turning exercises	
Group Five	Sevenths	22
	Scale patterns C, G and D	
	Contrapuntal studies	
Group Six	Octaves	25
	Octave hopping	
	Legato thirds	
Group Seven	Octaves and scale patterns	28
	Hand-over-hand techniques	
	Chord patterns	
	Crab exercise for keyboard geography	

GENERAL TECHNIQUE TIPS

1. Keep fingers curved and wrists level.

2. Lift curved fingers as high as possible and drop onto each note, maintaining a good legato or smooth connection between each note. Let the piano carry your hand.

3. Keep thumbs over the keyboard and the long fingers close to the black notes.

4. When playing the thumbs lift them to the level of the second joint in the knuckles and drop them at an angle always keeping the wrists level.

5. Angle elbows slightly out from the body.

6. When playing scale passages, pass the thumb under the third finger without altering the angle of the hand. Make sure thumb begins to turn under once the second finger has sounded the note, so that it will be in position in plenty of time.

7. Play each exercise slowly and evenly at first, gradually building up speed as the finger muscles gain strength.

8. Practise some of the exercises at varying tonal levels ranging from soft to very loud.

For more detailed information on basic piano technique refer to
Book 1A of the *Contemporary Piano Method*

TIME-VALUES

The number of counts each note receives can be shown by boxes drawn under the notes which can be coloured in to represent the duration of the sound. For an example of a completed colour chart refer to the *Contemporary Piano Method – Junior Primer*.

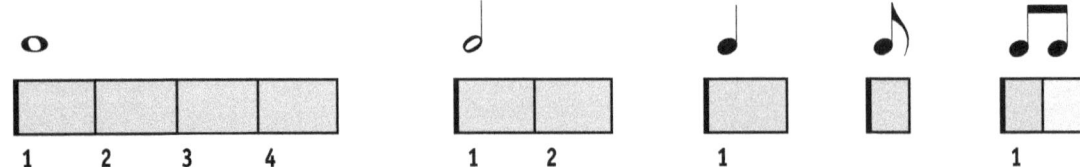

The boxes representing the rests are left as blank white space.

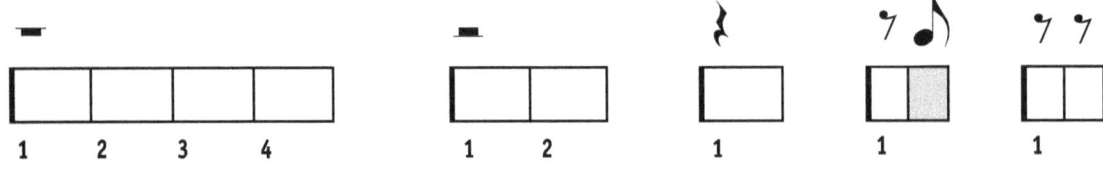

QUICK AND EASY RHYTHM TRAINING

THE COLOUR SYSTEM:

o - purple or mauve
♩ - dark blue or light blue
𝅗𝅥 - yellow or orange
♪ - red or pink

How to colour in the boxes
- Use alternating colours if more than one note of the same type appears in succession
- If a single note of one type occurs you may choose either of the given colours
- Dotted notes – extend the colour of the original note for half as long again
- Tied notes – choose the colour of the longer of the two notes for the entire combined length

Clapping
- For notes – hold hands together while the colour continues
- For rests – take hand apart and beat time in the air

When eighth notes are used in time signatures where the beat note is a quarter note, count them by saying 'AND' (+) on the second of each pair of eighth notes.

COLOUR THE BOXES AND THEN CLAP THE RHYTHMS

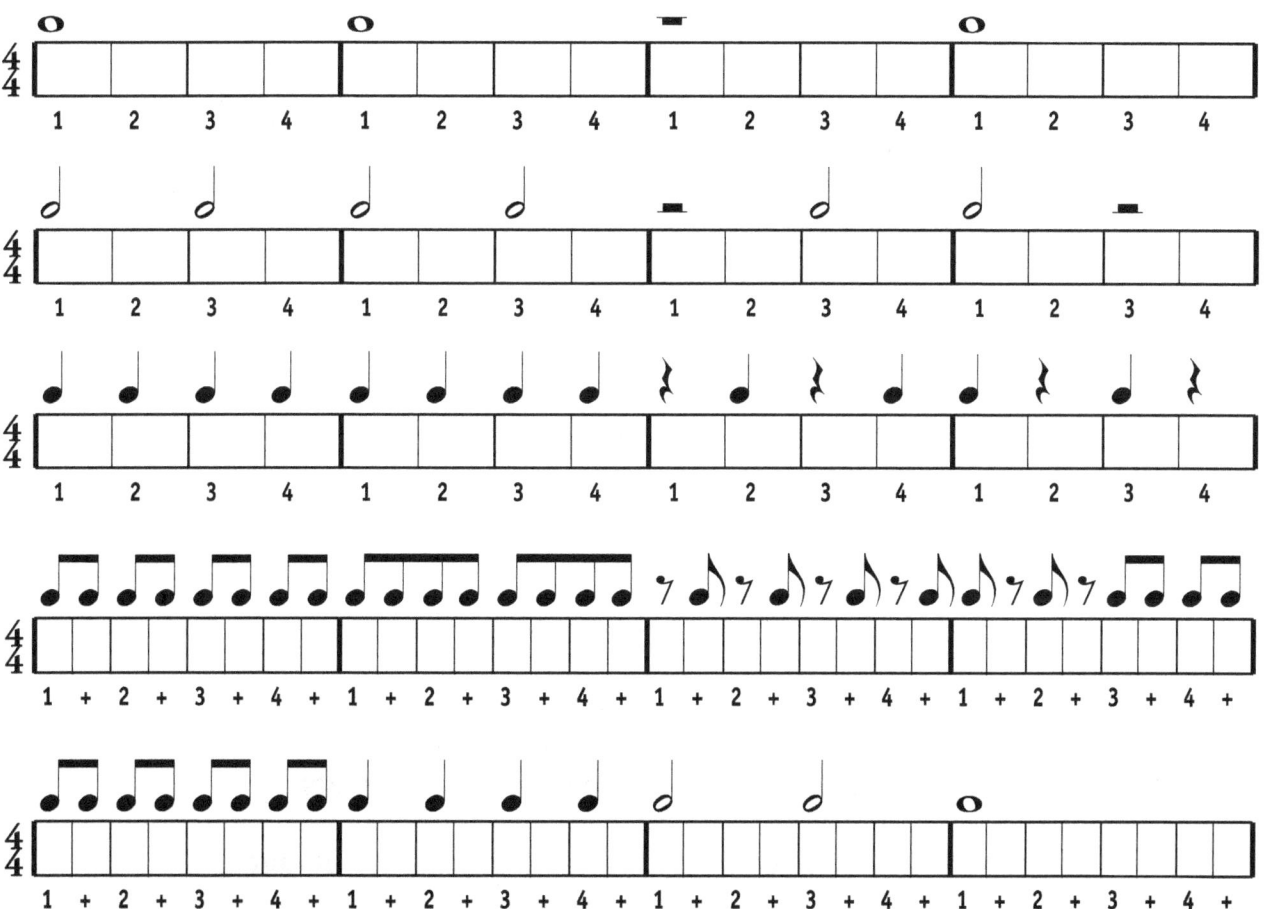

For information on the values of the notes and their names,
refer to *Book One* of the *Contemporary Theory Workbook* series.

GROUP ONE

Exercises using Steps (2nds)
in *similar* or *contrary motion*

Signpost Cs

Use the Cs as location points on the music and on the keyboard

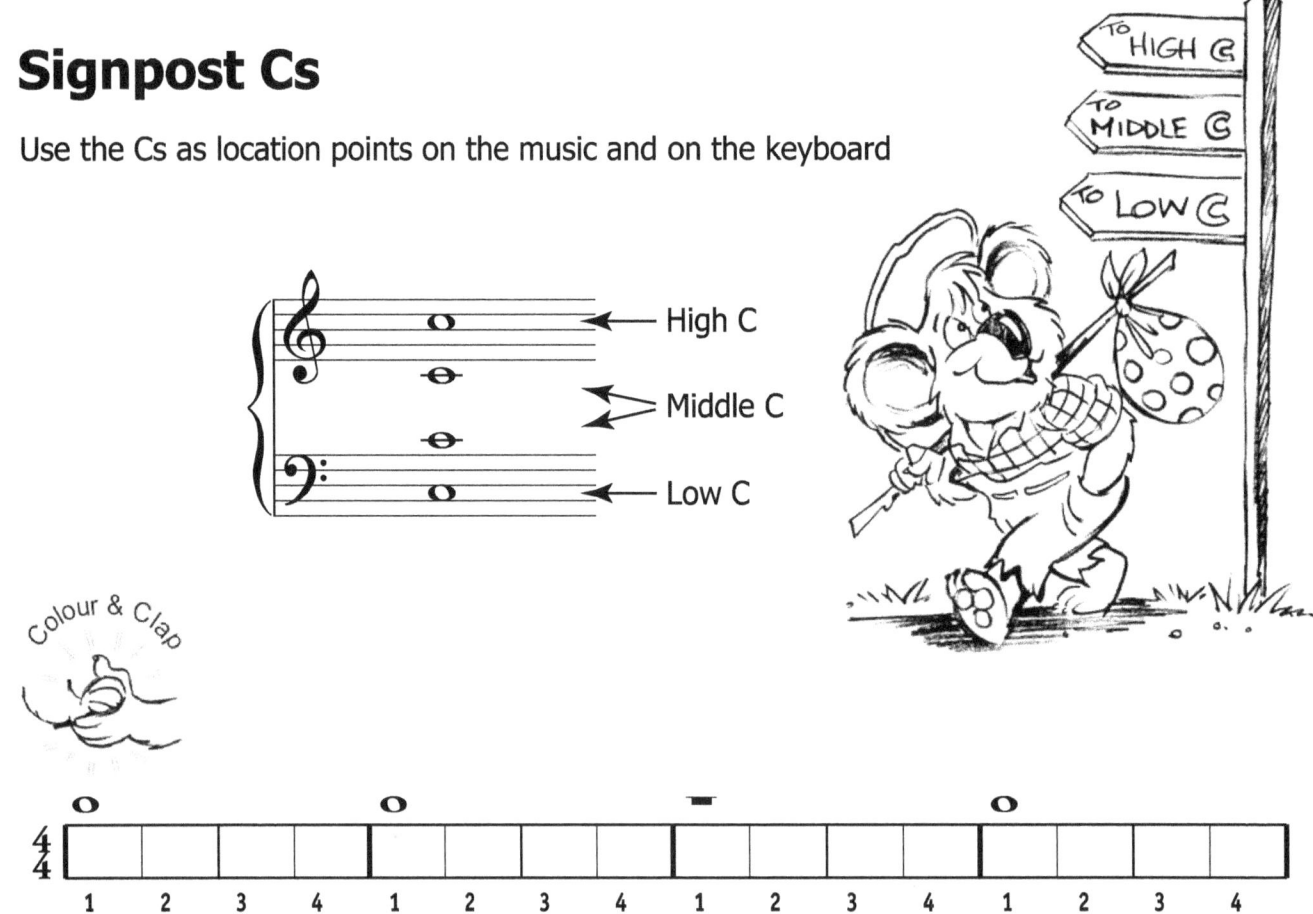

PRACTICE PROCEDURE

- Play each exercise separately before playing hands together

- Finger-trace the music as was done in the *Junior Primer* and as shown on the *Contemporary Piano Method* DVD

- Talk and or sing each exercise in the manner shown on the DVD

- When playing 'hands together', focus your eyes on the lower of the two staves
- This will enable you to see both staves, pay more attention to the left hand line and perceive the direction in which the music is moving for both parts

- Whenever possible, say the intervals and direction (**up, down, in, out** or **oblique**) and insert the counting

    Like this: **Step up** 2 3 4, **skip down** 2 3 4
      or **Step out** 2 **step out** 2, or **step in** 2 **step in** 2

Similar Motion
Hands together moving in the same direction – *up* or *down*

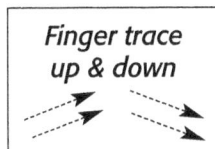

1. Level One – Play as written using the ***Signpost Cs*** as starting points
Level Two – Play this line transposed into other keys, using the **lower** end of the scale pattern

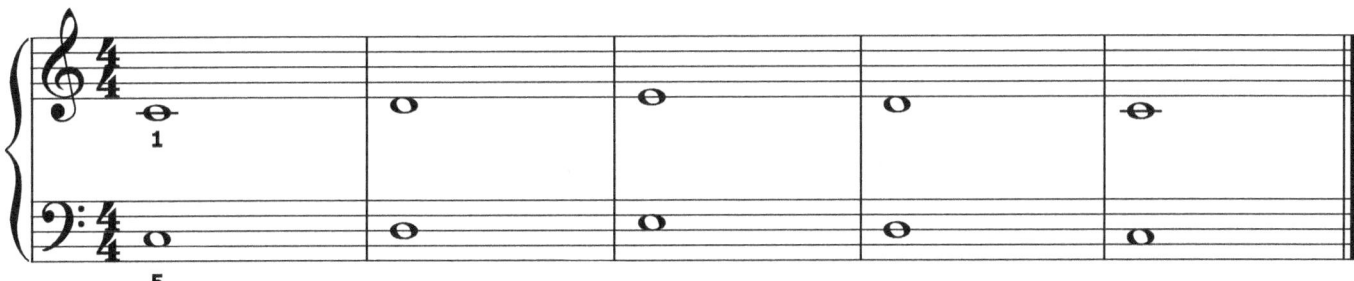

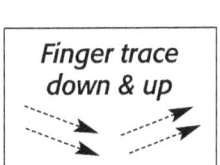

2. Level One – Play as written using the ***Signpost Cs*** as starting points
Level Two – Play this line transposed into other keys, using the **upper** end of the scale pattern

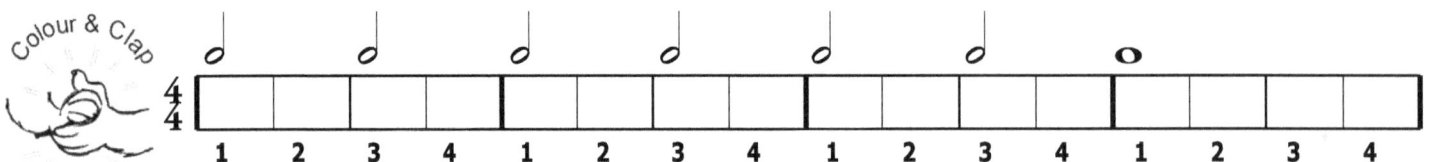

3.

4.

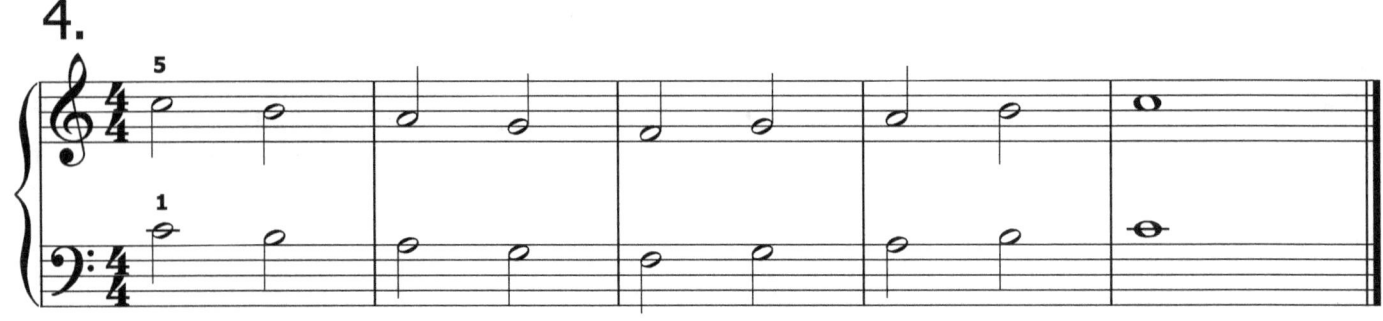

Contrary Motion
Hands moving in opposite directions - *out* **or** *in*

GROUP TWO

Exercises adding Skips (3rds) and Sames (primes)
and introducing ***eighth notes*** (quavers)

1.

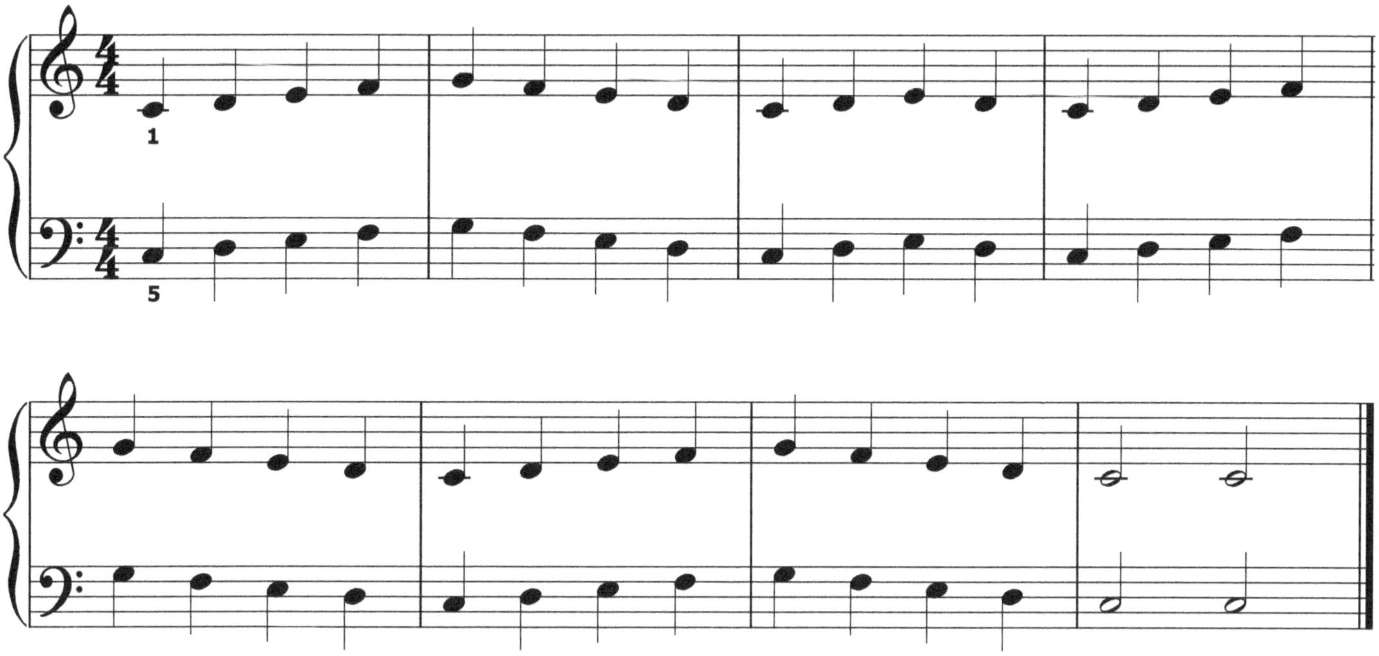

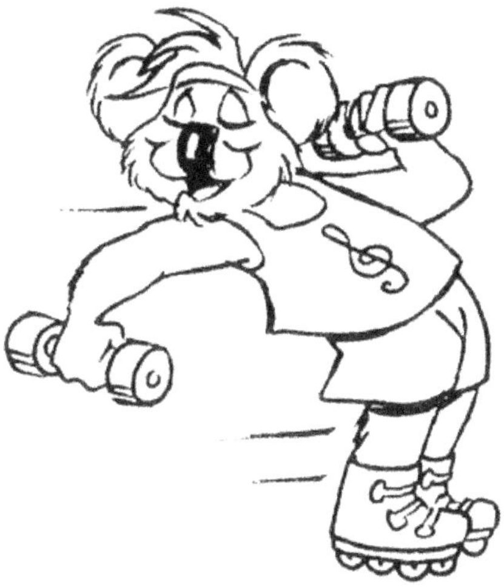

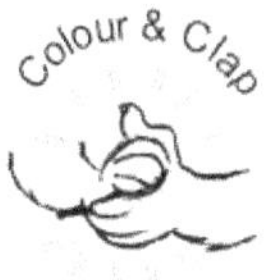

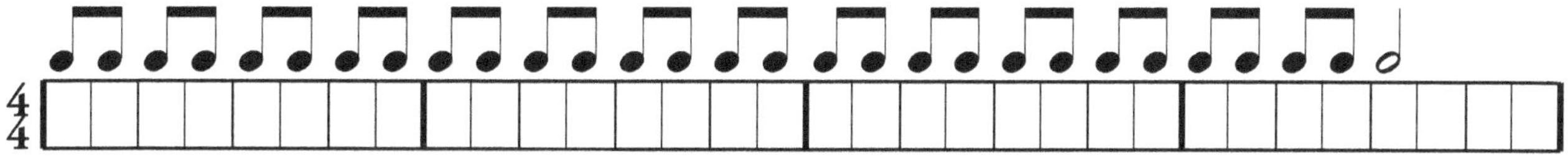

1 + 2 + 3 + 4 + 1 + 2 + 3 + 4 + 1 + 2 + 3 + 4 + 1 + 2 + 3 + 4 +

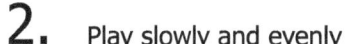

2. Play slowly and evenly

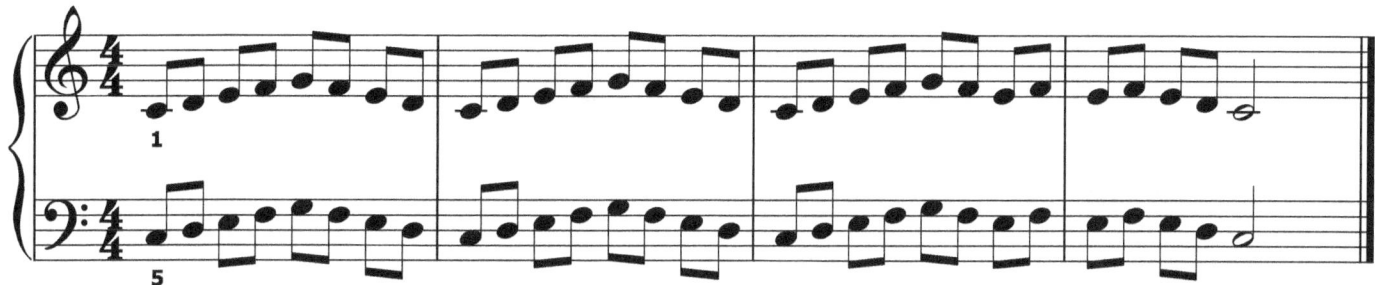

5.

6.
Treat the repeated quarter notes (crotchets) in the same manner as the eighth notes (quavers) in No.5

Play the Left Hand steps smoothly joined (legato)

7.
Play the Right Hand steps *legato*

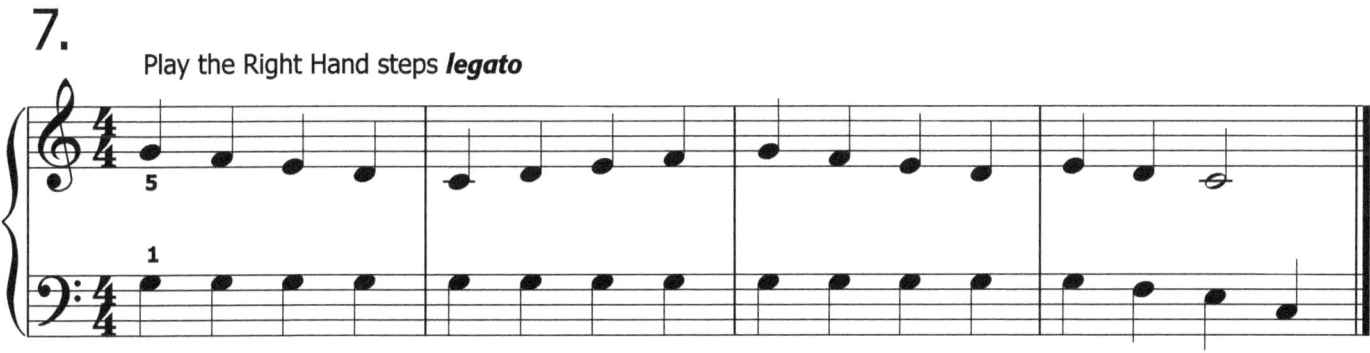

8.

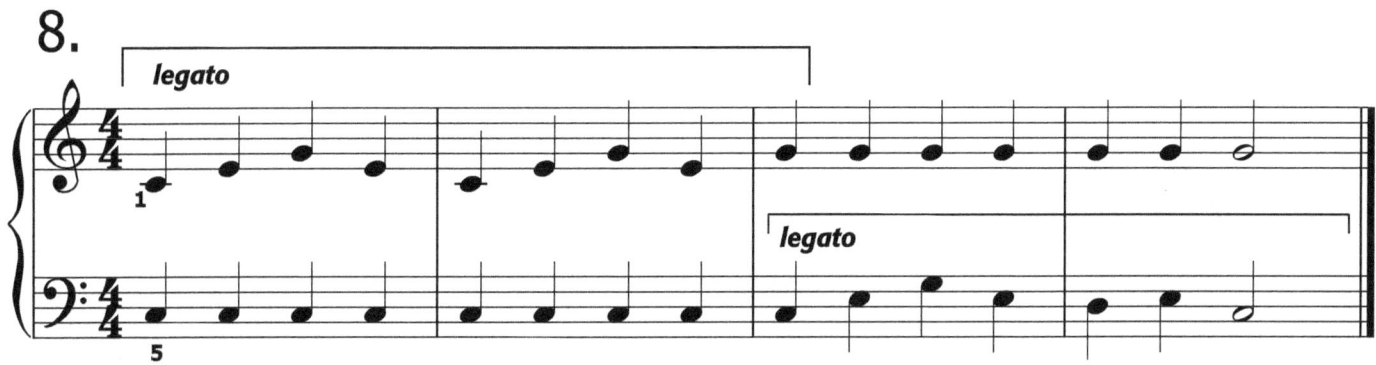

Harmonic Skips (3rds) and Root Position Triads

Staccato – detached

The strict interpretation of staccato is to play the notes half value.

- For this piece play all the quarter notes with a staccato touch in the same style as the eighth notes in No.5 of *Group Two*
- Play the half notes and whole notes full length

9. Staccato

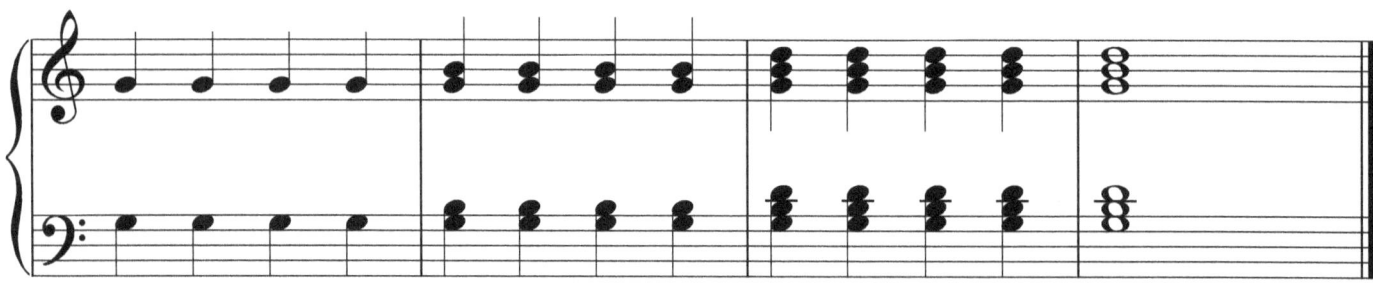

For more information on ***staccato touch***
Refer to CPM 1A p48

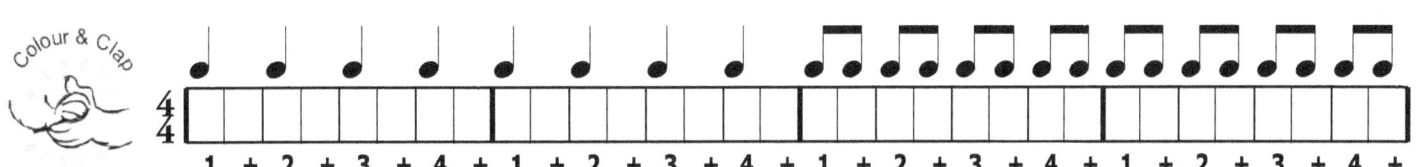

10. Decide on your speed for the **second** system* before commencing to play.

* A **system** is a set of staff lines for an instrument or a group of instruments.
  A piano system consists of a **treble staff** and a **bass staff** connected by a brace.
  It is also known as a **Great Staff** or **Grand Staff**.

GROUP THREE

Exercises adding Skip-plus-ones (4ths) and Jumps (5ths)

Before commencing this group make sure you know about C and G major scales
Refer to CPM 1A pp26-29, CTW Bk1 p35

1.

2. Level One – Play at the lower end of G Major scale (all white notes)
Level Two – Play this line transposed into other keys, using the **lower** end of the scale pattern

3.

4.

5. Play slowly

9. Dots above or below the note-head mean play with a ***staccato*** touch: detached.
Play in the same manner as the eighth notes (quavers) in Group 2 – No. 5.
Refer also to p48 in CPM1A

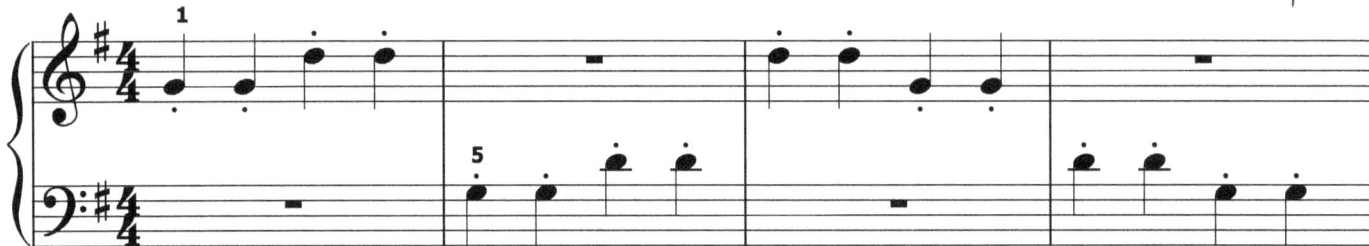

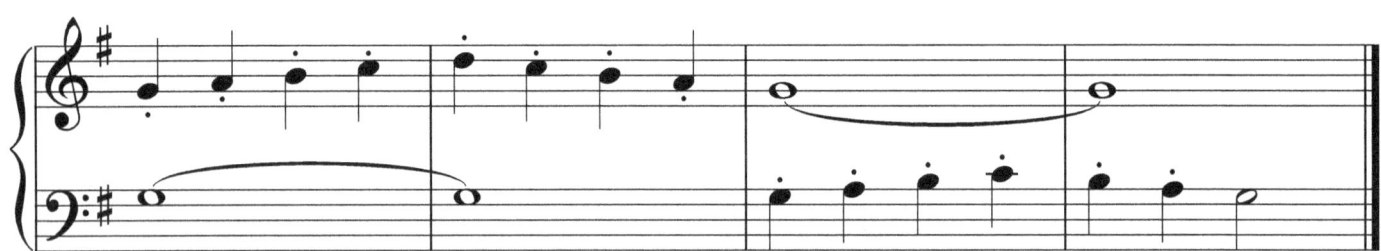

10.
- Play the quarter-note melodies smoothly (legato)
- Prepare to play the repeated minim value notes by lifting the finger on the count of 'and' after 2
  That is : 1 + 2 +

  (V = lift)
- Play all the other intervals smoothly

GROUP FOUR
Exercises adding Sixths and Scales

Refer to CPM 1A p39, CTP - p36-40 CTW Bk1 p42-44

Scales

Italian: *la scala* – the ladder

Refer to: Pictorial Patterns for Keyboard Scales and Chords

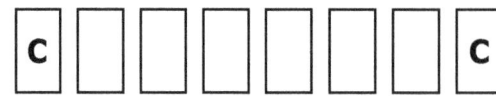

5. **Similar Motion**

6. **Similar Motion**

7. **Contrary Motion**

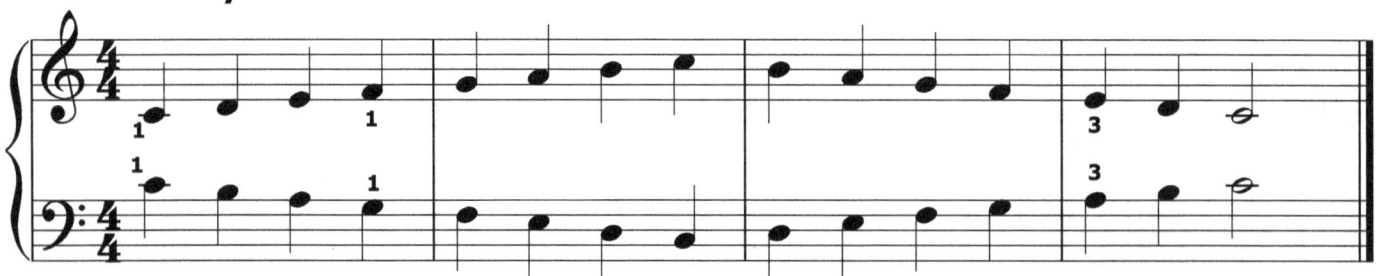

8. **Contrary Motion**

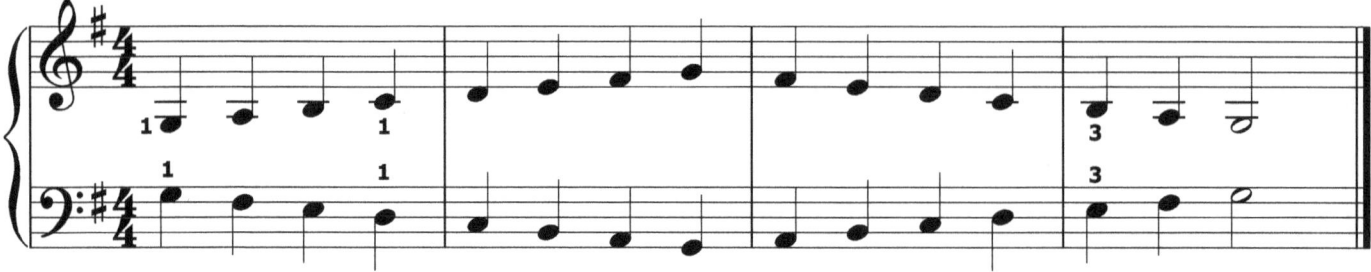

Thumb turning exercises
Refer to *Technique Tips* No. 6

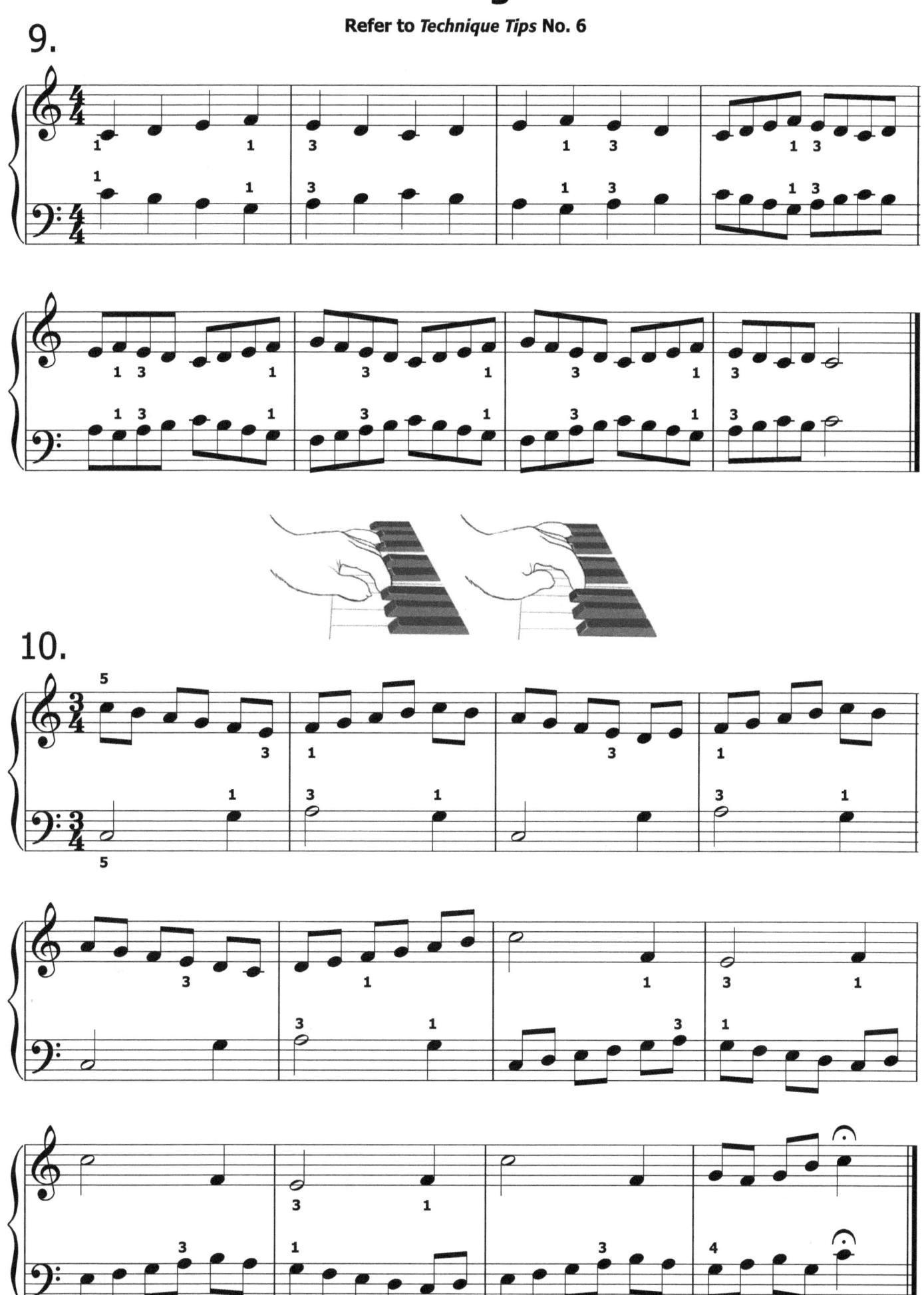

GROUP FIVE
Exercises adding Sevenths
Refer to CPM 1A p44, CTP p36-40, CTW Bk1 p42-44

1.

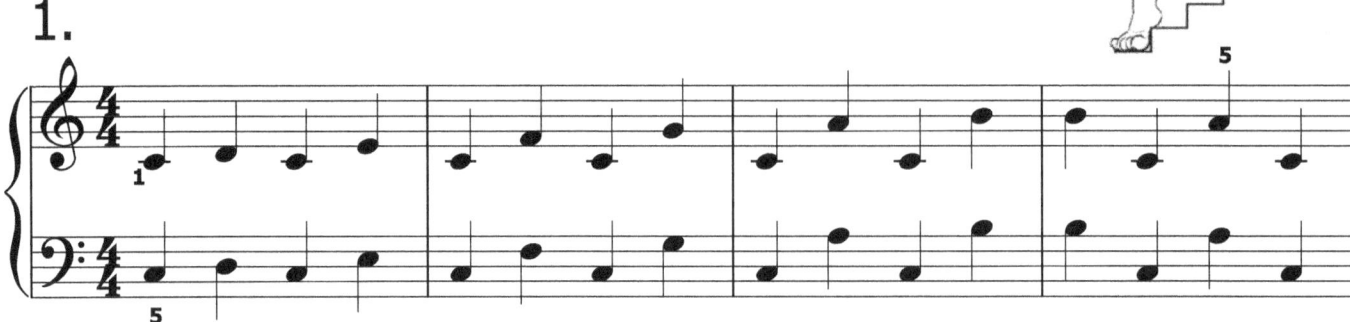

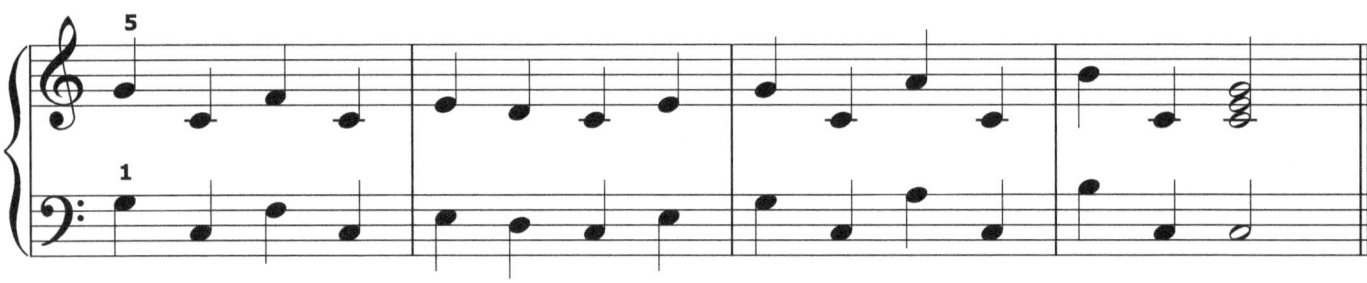

2. Move along the scale pathway for this key

3.

4.

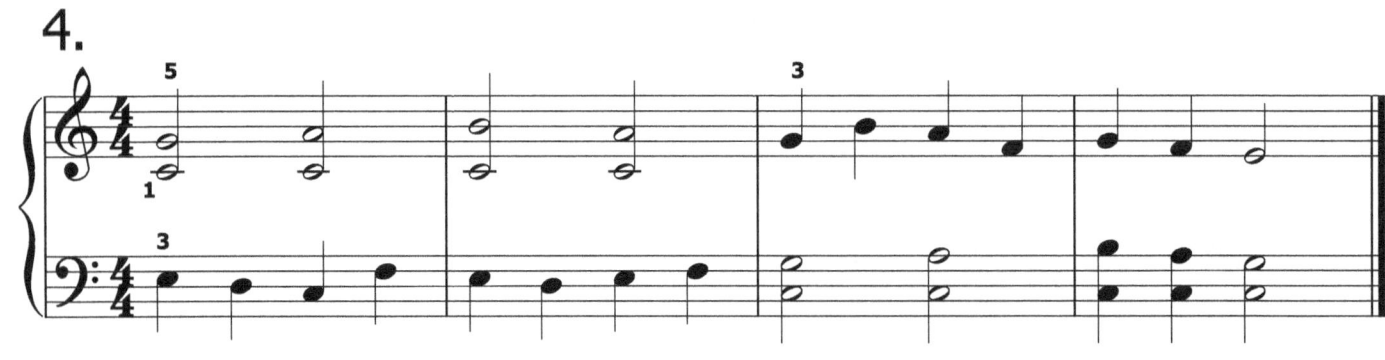

5. **Similar Motion**

6. **Contrary Motion**

7. **Lower section of scale pattern**: place fingers over the scale pattern keys before commencing
First time – play *legato* (smoothly connected)   Second time – play *staccato* (detached)

8. **Upper section of scale pattern**: place fingers over the scale pattern keys before commencing
First time – play all the eighth notes *legato*   Second time – play them *staccato*

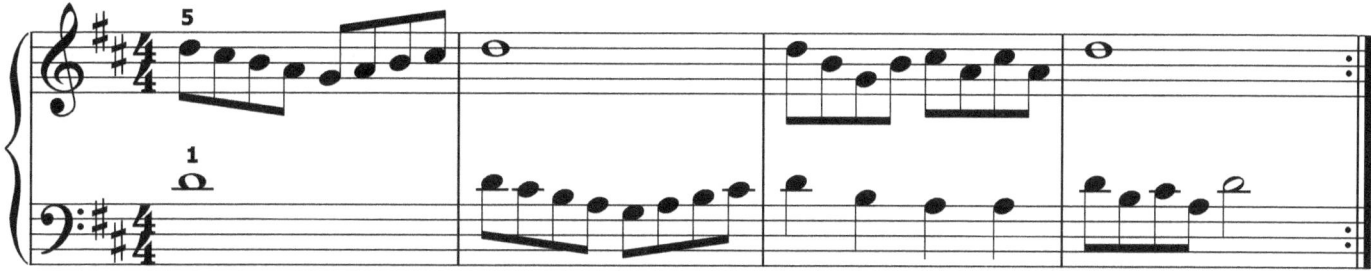

Part Playing or Contrapuntal Exercises

(***contrapuntal*** means point against point)

Right Hand plays — Soprano line, Alto line

Left Hand plays — Tenor line, Bass line

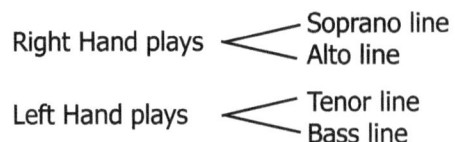

9. Lift fingers off the whole notes on the last 'a' of each bar to be ready to play the repeated note

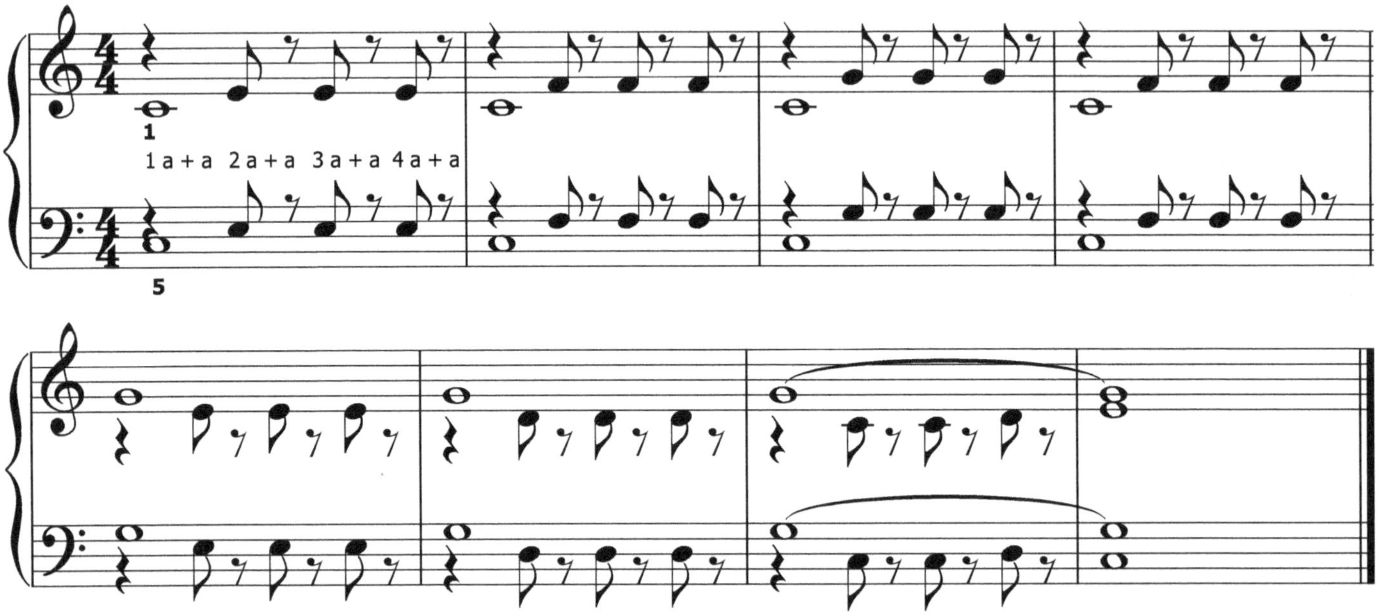

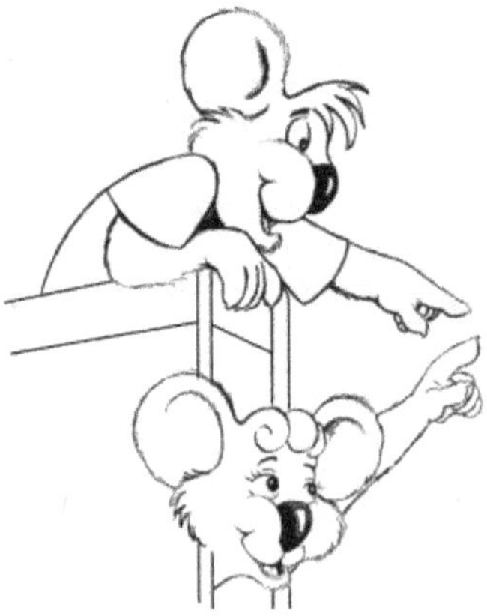

1
1 a + a 2 a + a 3 a + a 4 a + a
5

10. Connect all whole notes smoothly

1
5

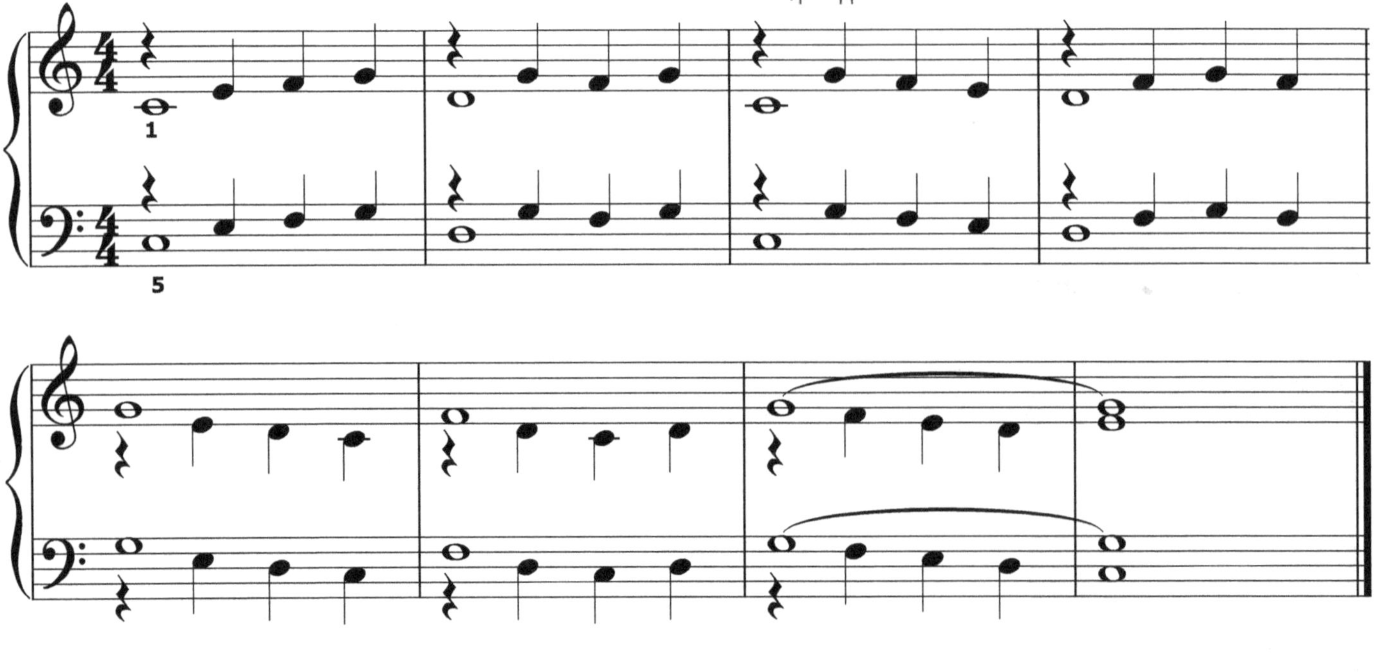

GROUP SIX
Exercises adding Octaves

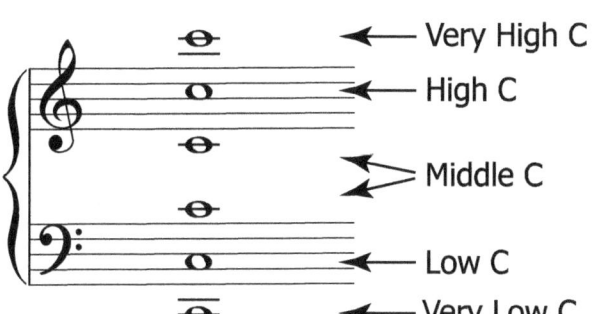

1. *Refer to CPM 1A p44, CTP p36-40, CTW Bk1 p42-44*

2. Small hands need play only the upper notes of the *harmonic octaves*

3. Octave hopping

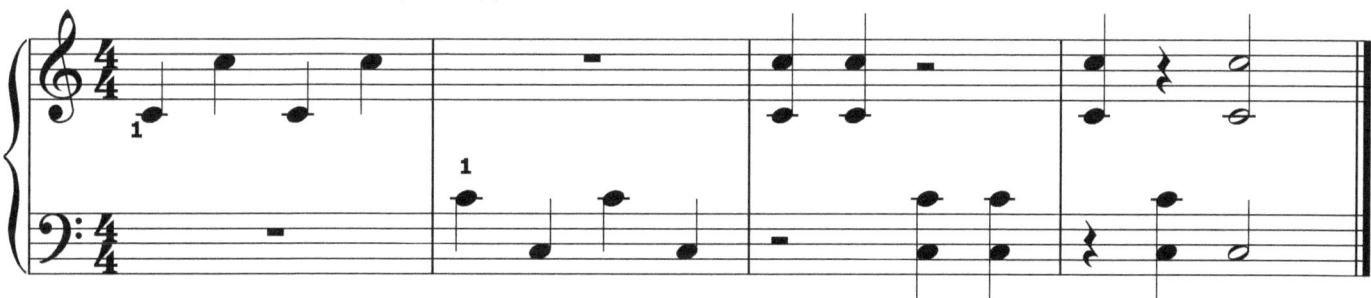
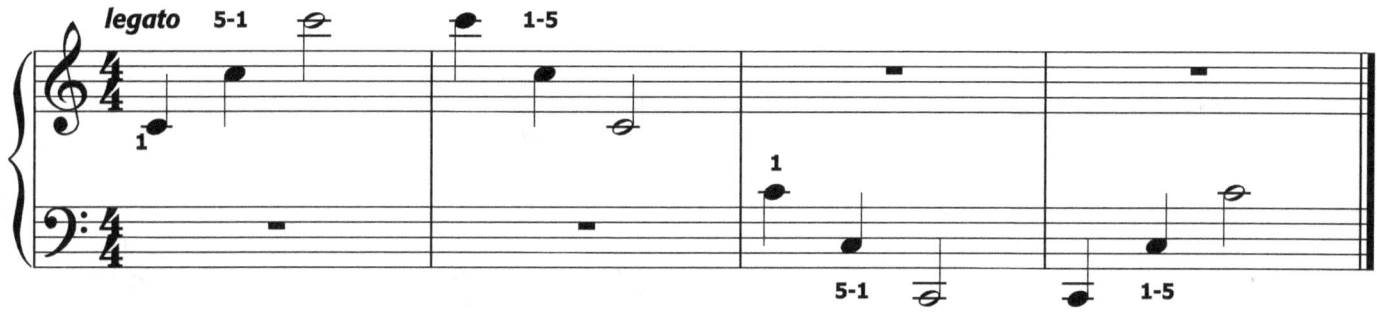

GROUP SEVEN
Exercises using Octaves, Chords, Scales and Hand-over-hand techniques

5.

Hand-over-hand exercises

(a) Right hand maintains position while left hand travels over

6.
- **Feel the distances between the hands**
- Measure the *left hand* descending octaves from your *right hand* thumb
- **Do not look down at your hands on the piano keys**

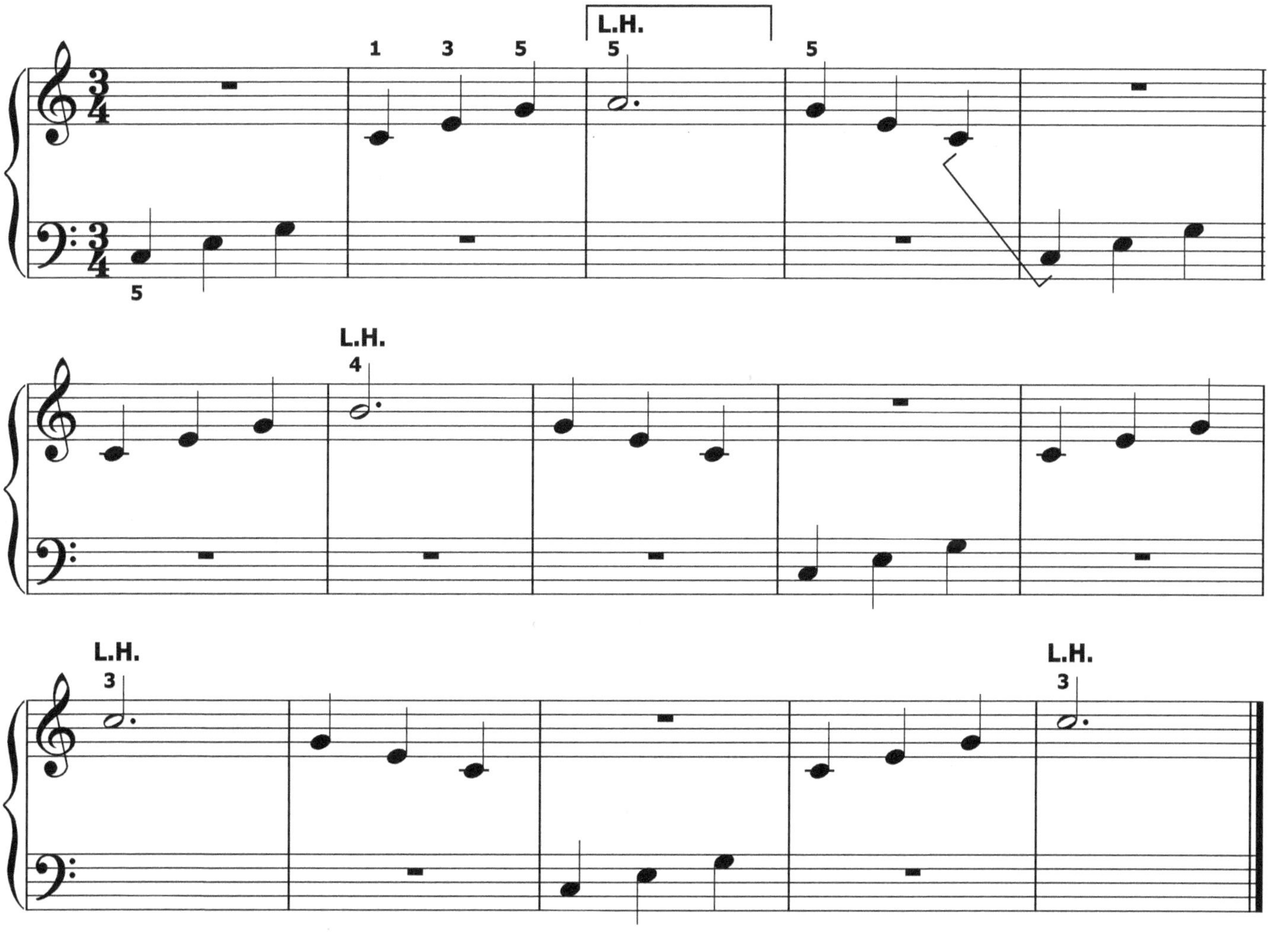

Hand-over-hand exercises

(b) Left hand maintains position while the right hand travels over

7.
- **Feel** the distances between the hands
- Measure the *right hand* ascending octaves from your *left hand* thumb
- **Do not look down at your hands on the piano keys**

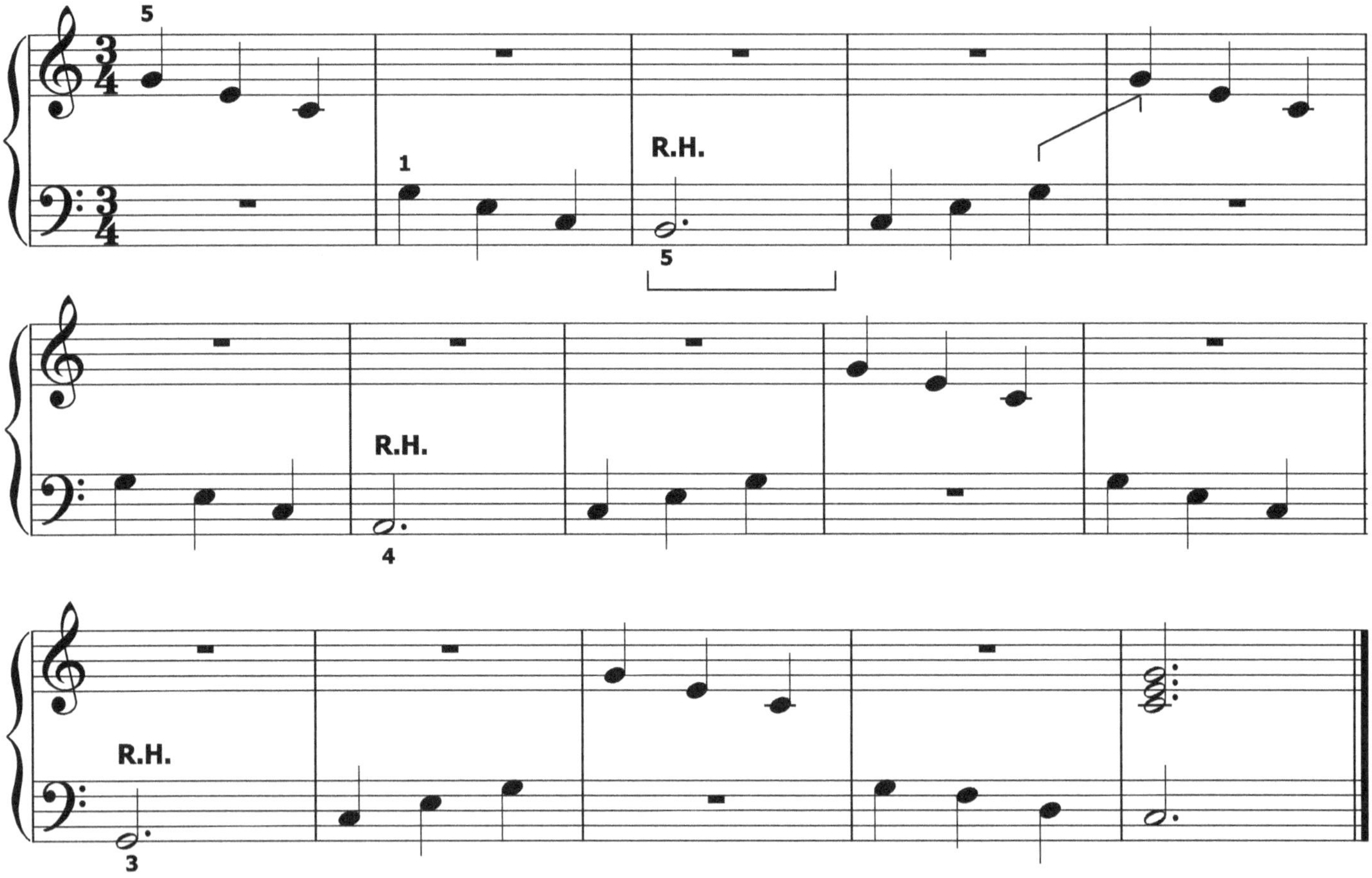

8. **Chord Climbing** – keep the chord shape in the hand and move the entire unit on the eighth note count indicated by the **'V'**

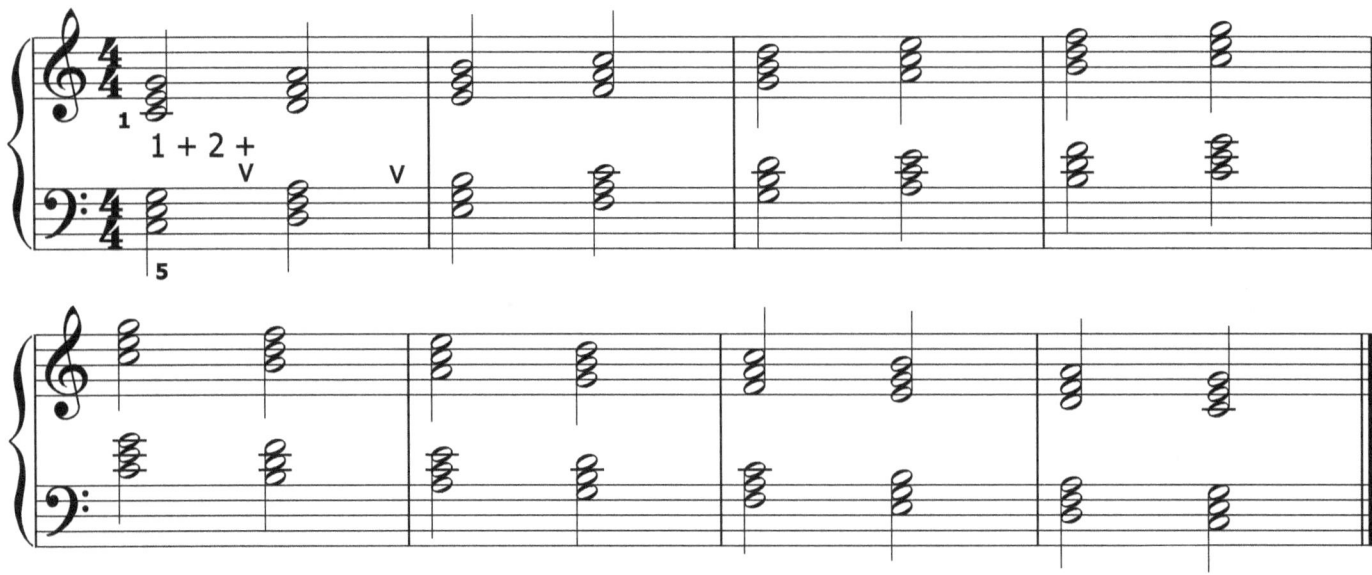

CRAB EXERCISE – COVERING ALL SEVEN POSITIONS OF THE MAJOR SCALE

11.
- Slide all five fingers onto the next position swapping each finger onto the next note
- Keep track of the sharp as each position is reached
- Transpose this to several keys

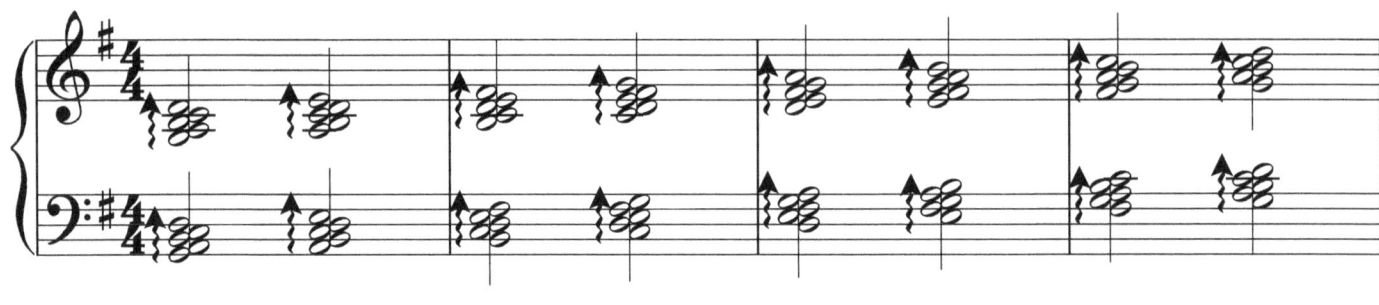

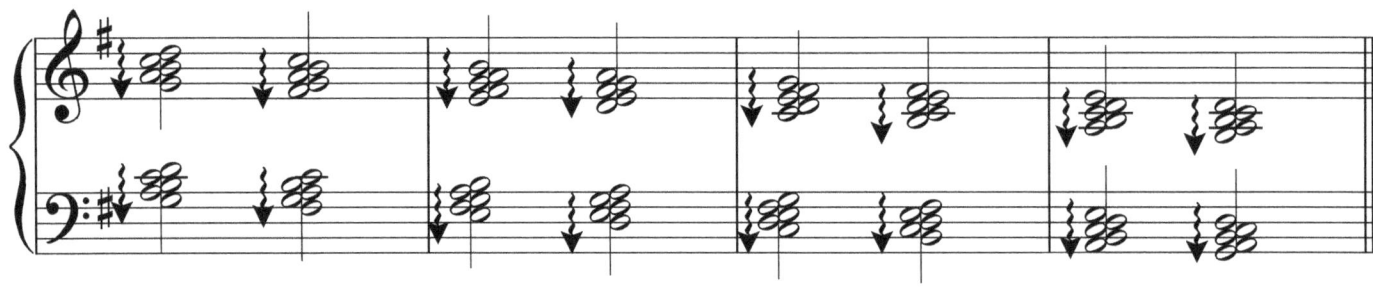

12.
- Play these two bar patterns on each of the eight scale positions shown in No.11
- Play hands separately as well as together

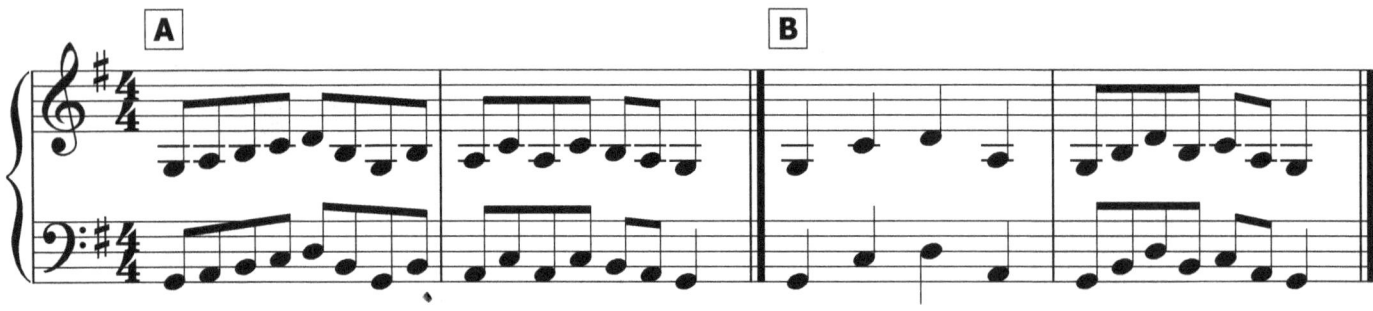

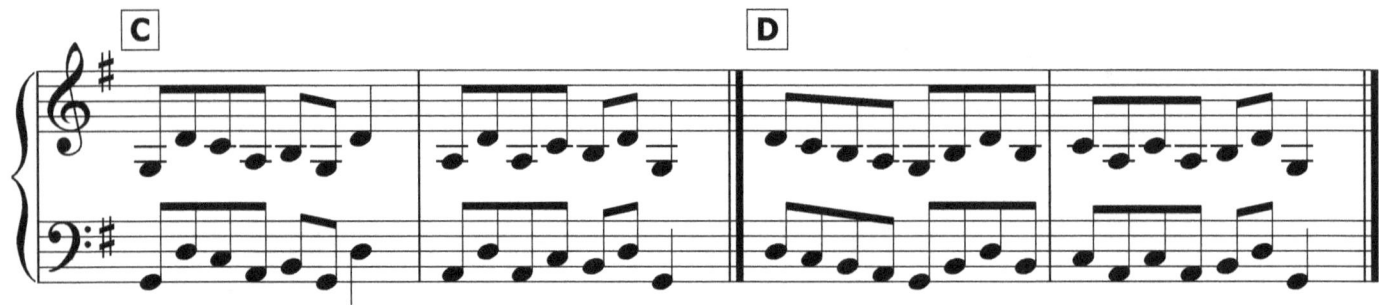

www.ingramcontent.com/pod-product-compliance
Lightning Source LLC
Chambersburg PA
CBHW080855090426
42734CB00013B/2998